Anita Ganeri

Published 2011 by
A&C Black Publishers Ltd.
36 Soho Square, London, W1D 3QY

www.acblack.com

ISBN HB 978-1-4081-3360-6
PB 978-1-4081-3361-3

A CIP catalogue for this book is available from the British Library.

Produced for A&C Black by Calcium. www.calciumcreative.co.uk

Printed and bound in China by C&C Offset Printing Co.

Acknowledgements

The publishers would like to thank the following for their kind permission to reproduce their photographs:

Cover: Shutterstock
Pages: Corbis: DLILLC 20, Chris Sattlberger 18, Kevin Schafer 12; Dreamstime: Anky 9, C L Chang 19, Eric Gevaert 8, Twikieartcat 16; Photolibrary: Mark MacEwan 21, Stan Osolinski 15, Cyril Ruoso 14; Shutterstock: Sima 17, Eric Isselée 6, Tim Jenner 3, 5, LiteChoices 4, Uryadnikov Sergey 10, Szefei 7, Charles Taylor 1, 11, Ly Dinh Quoc Vu 13.

Contents

My Story

I am an orangutan. I used to live in the **rainforest**, but now I live in a **rescue centre**. This is my story.

All about me

I am a type of **ape**, like chimpanzees and gorillas. I have a large body, long, strong arms and I'm covered in shaggy red-brown hair.

I am a brilliant climber.

Forest man

The name 'orangutan' means 'man of the forest' in Malaysian.

Lots of hair

High life

Orangutans live high up in rainforest trees – they don't often go down to the ground.

My Home

I used to live in a rainforest on a big island called Borneo, in Asia. I lived there with lots of other orangutans.

Jungle swinger

I lived high up in the trees and I used to swing from branch to branch, using my long arms. I held on tightly with my strong hands and feet.

Even baby orangutans have long arms.

Extra long

An orangutan has very long arms – they are two times as long as its legs!

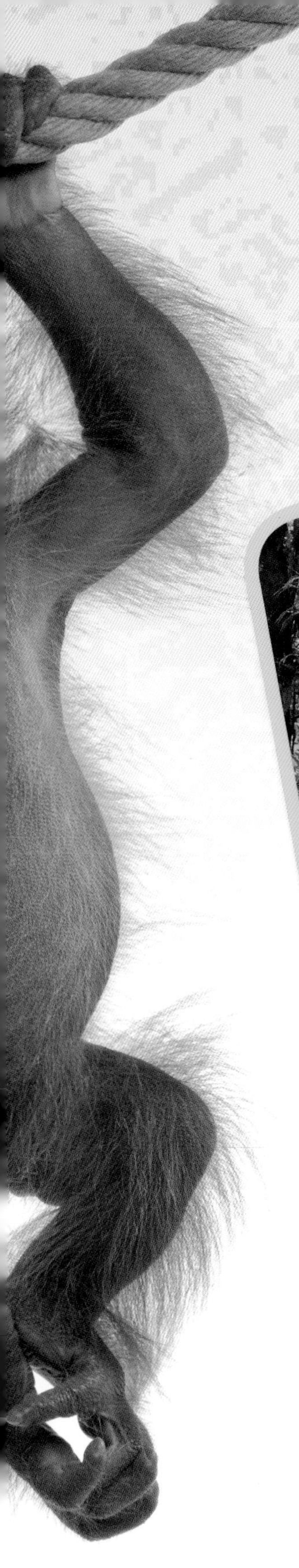

Rainforests

Rainforests are thick forests that grow in warm parts of the world. Millions of animals live in them.

Early Days

I was born in a **nest** in the rainforest trees. After that I lived with my mother. She looked after me until I was old enough to care for myself.

What about my dad?

My father did not live with us. **Male** orangutans stay on their own – they don't like it if other orangutans come too close.

Fights

Orangutan males sometimes fight each other over food and females.

I rode on my mum's back.

Stay away

Males puff up their throats to make a loud noise which tells other orangutans to stay away.

Good Morning

When I lived in the rainforest, I woke up early in the morning to look for breakfast. I usually had fruit – my favourite food!

Lunch time

Next I looked for food for lunch. There were lots of things to eat in the forest, from leaves to tree bark and plant roots. I even ate flowers, too.

Forest food

Orangutans must travel all over the rainforest to find enough food.

Orangutans pick fruit from trees.

What's for tea?

Orangutans look for food with their mums until they are eight years old. After that, they feed themselves.

Favourite Foods

Of all the rainforest fruit, I liked **durian** fruit the best. I picked it from trees, then I peeled it with my lips and teeth.

Thirsty work

When I felt thirsty, I scooped up some water from a hole in a tree. It rains a lot in the rainforest, so there was plenty of water to drink.

I ate lots of different fruit in the rainforest.

On the menu

Orangutans also eat seeds, insects, honey, and eggs.

Durian
fruit

Tastes good

These prickly durian fruit smell horrible, but they taste delicious.

Making a Nest

At night, I slept in a nest in the trees. My mother made the nest from branches and leaves – she made a new nest every night.

Making my nest

When I got older, my mother showed me how to make a nest. First I bent some big branches over, then I stuck in twigs and leaves. It took a lot of **practice**.

Take a nap

Orangutans also make a day nest to nap in during the day.

Keeps raining

It rains every day in the rainforest, so orangutans use leafy branches as umbrellas.

I loved sleeping in my nest.

Disaster Strikes!

Then one day, something terrible happened – our home was destroyed! It began early in the morning, with a loud buzzing noise.

Cutting down trees

People called loggers were cutting down our trees. As the noise of their machines got closer, I became terrified. Then the tree next to ours crashed to the ground!

I was so scared, I gripped onto mum.

Precious trees

Loggers cut down trees to clear the land for growing **crops**.

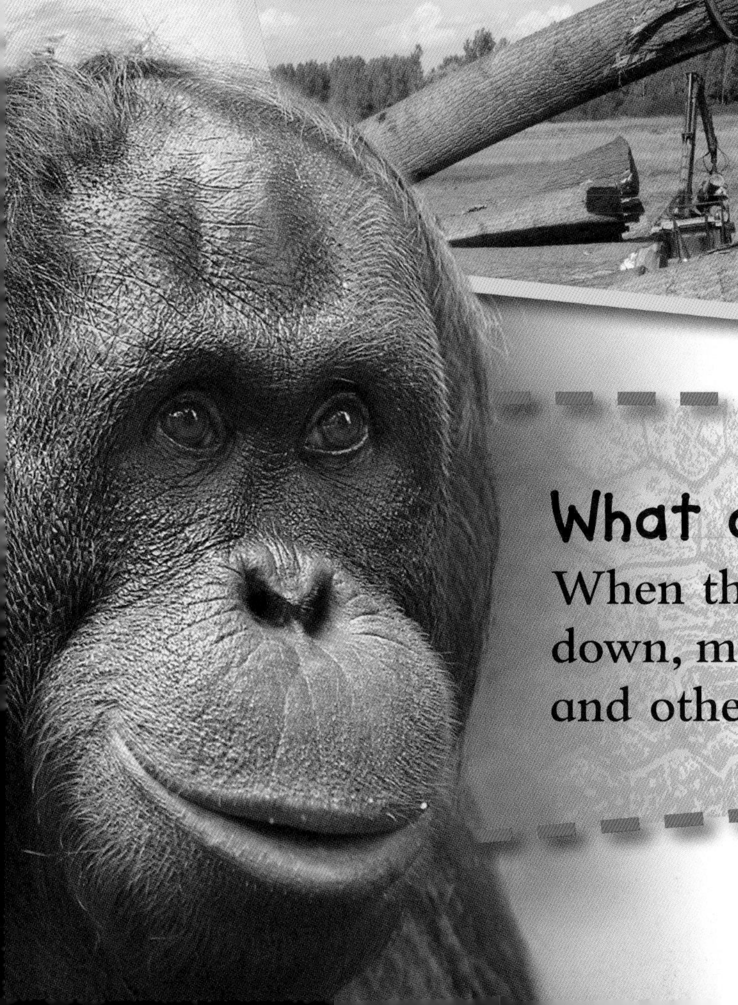

What about us?

When the forest is cut down, many orangutans and other animals die.

Danger

When the loggers began to cut our tree, I grabbed onto mum. She swung from one tree to the next until we were far away.

No more trees

We reached the edge of the rainforest where there were no more trees, so mum dropped onto the ground. But we were not out of danger yet – a woman grabbed me and put me in a cage.

Hungry orangutans

Even orangutans that survive in the jungle are still not safe. Without trees, they cannot find enough to eat. If they eat the crops grown on forest land, the farmers kill them.

The future

If people don't stop chopping down the rainforests, a zoo may one day be the only place where you can see orangutans.

Rainforest

Farmland

Our home has become **farmland**.

Rescued

Luckily, the woman who put me in the cage was helping me – she took me to a rescue centre. My mother was taken to the rescue centre, too. We are safe here.

Back to the wild

The rescue centre will look after us until we can go back to the forest. Then we shall live like we did before.

We like the rescue centre but we want to live wild.

Babies

Rescue centre workers take care of **orphaned** orangutan babies and teach them how to survive in the wild.

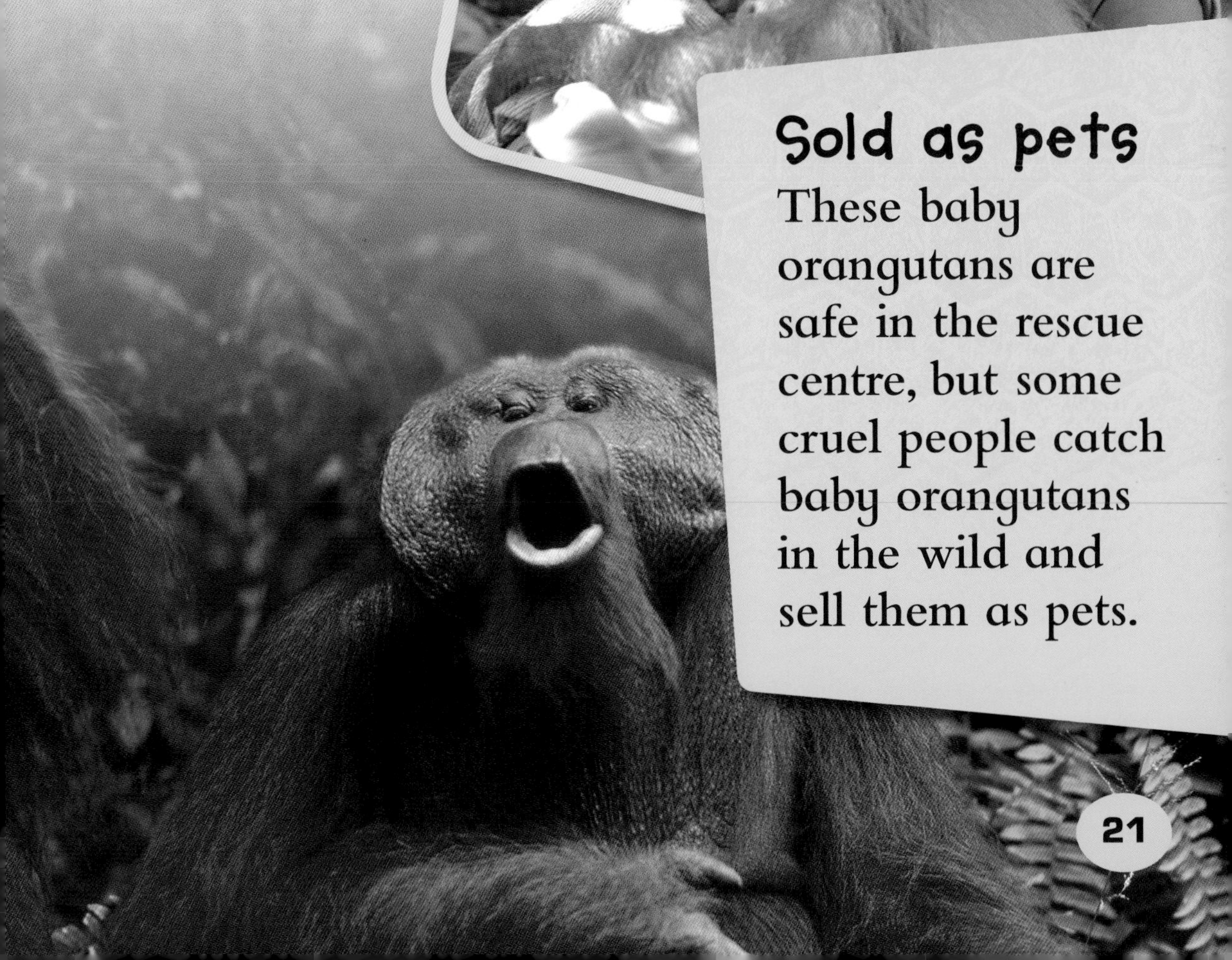

Sold as pets

These baby orangutans are safe in the rescue centre, but some cruel people catch baby orangutans in the wild and sell them as pets.

Glossary

Asia large area of the world, also called a continent

ape animal group that includes orangutans, gorillas, and chimpanzees

crops plants that are grown for food

durian type of rainforest fruit

farmland land where animals are kept and plants are grown for food

male not female. In humans males can be boys or men.

nest place where an animal sleeps and raises its young

orphaned when an animal or person's parents are killed. An orphan has no mother or father.

practice doing something over and over again

rainforest forest where the weather is warm and wet all year round

rescue centre place where animals are looked after

Further Reading

Websites

Follow an orangutan through the day at:
www.kids.nationalgeographic.com/kids/animals/creaturefeature/orangutan

Find out more about orangutans in Sumatra and in Borneo at:
www.orangutans-sos.org/kids/orangutan_facts

Learn more about rescued orangutans in Borneo at:
www.savetheorangutan.org.uk

Books

Animal Lives: Orangutans
by Sally Morgan, QED (2007).

Rainforest Animals: Orangutans
by Anita Ganeri, Raintree (2010).

Why are Orang-utans So Hairy? by
Camilla de la Bédoyère, Miles Kelly (2008).

Index